BOB WILLS & HIS TEXAS PLAYBOYS

Voice • Piano • Guitar

Special thanks to the following
for their help with this special project.
Lee Ross, Betty Kissell, Edna Kissell,
Gene Bear, Bobby Koefer, Leonard Moss
and Cindy Walker.

Catalog #07-1047

ISBN# 1-56922-106-5

Printed in the United States of America

Produced by John L. Haag

Exclusive Distributor:
CREATIVE CONCEPTS PUBLISHING CORPORATION
6020-B Nicolle Street, Ventura, California 93003

Check out our Web site at *http://www.creativeconcepts.com* or you can Email us at *mail@creativeconcepts.com*

CONTENTS

CONTENTS

THE BOB WILLS LEGACY

James Robert Wills was born on a farm in Limestone County, East Texas, on March 6, 1905. During his long career as a musician and bandleader, he was to organize one of the finest stage and recording bands ever to perform country music, develop his personal talents as a fiddler and singer, and originate what would come to be recognized as one of the major sub-styles of the country music traditions: Western Swing. Over nearly four decades, Bob Wills was to develop a fanatical following for himself and his "Texas Playboys" in his native Southwest. His repertory and performance style contributed many innovative elements to country music, for much of what is heard today under the "country" heading can be traced to musical influences generated by Bob Wills.

But Bob Wills' most famous stylistic trademark is perhaps the energetic "Ahh ha" which punctuates his musical personality. He said this vocal signature dates back to his grandfather, as well as the spontaneous commentary which he invariably would insert between the established lines between each verse. This technique was central to the base of his popularity, for it took much of the stiffness out of structured music and put it on much more personal terms.

The number of musicians in the Texas Playboys (the name Bob bestowed upon his band) varied, down through the years, from ten to twenty-two. Bob was actually the first to assemble an orchestra (or, if you prefer, big band) to play country music, and he was also instrumental in introducing horns and drums to the genre. The fiddles, however, were always the central point of any Bob Wills band. They became his trademark, and made up the first "string section" in country music.

For the record, Bob's basic band included: Tommy Duncan (vocals), Leon McAuliff (steel guitar), Everett Stover (trumpet), Zeb McNally (sax), Smokey Ducas (drums), Herman Arnspiger (guitar), Sleepy Johnson and Al Stricklin (piano) and many other outstanding musicians too numerous to mention.

Before his death in 1975, Bob Wills lived to see an incredible revival of his music among a new generation of fans and talented, young musicians. His repertory and style are currently being revitalized by many artists including Willie Nelson, Waylon Jennings, Merle Haggard, John Denver, Asleep At The Wheel, Commander Cody, Charlie Daniels and many, many others.

One of Bob's last public appearances was in 1968, when he was initiated as a member of the prestigious Country Music Hall of Fame in Nashville. There is really no way that Bob could ever be paid back in full for the contribution he made to country music and the happiness which his music brought to millions of people, but the honor was just one way of saying a "thank-you" which defies words.

His plaque reads:

> "Grandson and son of champion fiddlers, he quickly established himself king of western swing. His famous trademark 'Ahh ha, take it away, Leon.' Entered radio with Lightcrust Doughboys in '29. Formed Texas Playboys in the 30's. Wrote and recorded "San Antonio Rose." Appeared in 26 Hollywood pictures. A living legend whose roadmap has charted new pathways into the world of American stage, radio, TV, records and movies."

Bob Wills was an innovator. He developed an entirely new style of music and built a huge following playing that "western swing" throughout Texas and the entire southwest. He took creativity to extremely high levels with hits like "San Antonio Rose" and generated so much excitement that even today, nearly 30 years after many of the selections in this book were first recorded, you can still find Bob Wills and his Texas Playboys on the radio all around the country.

We hope you will enjoy the songs in this collection which are truly the very best from Bob Wills "The King of Western Swing"!

Bob Wills and his Texas Playboys, Los Angeles, 1944. Standing left to right: Everett Stover, Louis Tierney, Tommy Duncan, Laura Lee Owens, Bob Wills, Cameron Hill, Tiny Mott. Kneeling: Les Anderson, Jimmy Wyble, Rip Ramsey, Monte Mountjoy, Millard Kelso.

Bob Wills

Bob Wills with his 157-year-old Guadagnini violin, 1943.

At the Pacific Square Ballroom in San Diego, 1943.

Luke Wills, Harley Huggins, Bob Wills, Joe Holly, Russell Hayden, Kelso, Leon McAuliffe.

Bob Wills, 1945.

Russell Hayden, Dub Taylor, Bob Wills.

Bob Wills (left) and Spade Cooley.

Bob Wills and some of his Texas Playboys at an outdoor radio broadcast, 1936. Left to right: Herman Arnspiger, guitar; Bob Wills, fiddle; Sleepy Johnson, vocals; unidentified saxophonist; Tommy Duncan, vocals; Everett Stover, trumpet; Zeb McNally, saxophone; Joe Ferguson, unidentified guitarist.

Bob Wills and his Texas Playboys at an early-morning rehearsal, about 1937. Left to right: Everett Stover, trumpet; Zeb McNally, saxophone; Leon McAuliffe; Alan Franklin, announcer; Tiny Mott, saxophone; Herman Arnspiger; Al Sticklin; Joe Ferguson; Bob Wills, fiddle; Smokey Dacus; Tommy Duncan; Son Lansford, bass; Sleepy Johnson, tenor banjo.

Signing the contract to make eight movies for Columbia Pictures in 1942. Left to right: David Randolph Milsten, Bob Wills, O. W. Mayo.

Bob Wills, about 1942.

Bob Wills at the door of his makeshift dressing room on location during the filming of a Columbia picture, 1942.

Bob Wills & His Texas Playboys, Trianon Ballroom, Oklahoma City, Oklahoma, 1950. Left to right: Bobby Koefer, steel guitar; Wayne Nichols, trumpet; Vern Harris, bus driver & doorman; Johnny Gimble, fiddle & electric mandolin; Red Norman, sax; Bob Wills, fiddle; Billy Houch, drums; Snuffy Smith, bass & body guard; Jack Loyd, bass & vocalist; Sheldon Bennett, guitar; Pee Wee Linn, piano; Eldon Shamblin, guitar & manager.

Maybe Bob Wills' hottest band. This California version of the Texas Playboys in 1944 or 1945 had some of Wills' most jazzy and experimental musicians. In the back row, left to right: Jack McElroy, announcer; Joe-Blow Galbreath, Bob's bodyguard; Billy Jack Wills; Rip Ramsey; Millard Kelso, super yodeler; first Texas Playgirl, Laura Lee; and Tommy Duncan. In the front row: Noel Boggs; Joe Holley; Louis Tierney; Bob Wills; Jimmy Wyble and Cameron Hill.

Bob Wills beside the plaque marking his election to the Country Music Hall of Fame.

Bing Crosby and Bob Wills in Hollywood, early 1940.

Luke Wills, Betty Kissell, Johnnie Lee Wills.

Glen Duncan and Tommy Duncan.

From left to right: Dean McKinney, Herb Remington, Evelyn McKinney, Louis Tierney, Johnny Cuviello, Bob Wills, Ocie Stockard, Billy Jack Wills, Tiny Moore, Millard Kelso, Eldon Shamblin, Tommy Duncan and fans.

Luke Wills.

The Wills Band, 1947. Kneeling, left to right: Ocie Stockard, Junior Barnard, Tommy Duncan, Millard Kelso, Monte Mountjoy. Standing: Bob Wills, Billy Jack Wills, Herb Renington, Tiny Moore, Luke Wills, Joe Holley, Eldon Shamblin.

Bob Wills and his Playboys, the original group, 1933. Left to right: June Whalin, Kermit Whalin, Bob Wills, Johnnie Lee Wills, Tommy Duncan, Everett Stover.

Ernie Ball and Tommy Duncan.

ACROSS THE ALLEY FROM THE ALAMO

Words and Music by Joe Greene

Easy Swing

A - cross the al - ley from the Al - a - mo, ___ Lived a

pin - to po - ny and a Na - va - jo, ___ { Who sang a sort of In - di - an
Who used to bake fri - jol - es in

Hi - de - ho ___ to the peo - ple pass - ing by. ___ The
corn - meal dough ___ for the peo - ple pass - ing by. ___ They

14

ALL NIGHT LONG

Words and Music by Bob Wills and Johnny Gimble

Fast country, with a "2" feel

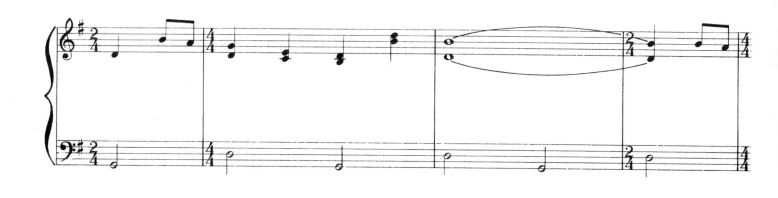

Ev - ery Sat - ur -day, long__
(See additional lyrics)

__ a-bout now, I feed my chick-ens and my milk-ing cow. Air's__

To Coda

__ fill-in' up with mus-ic and song. Gon-na have a par-ty

18

Additional Lyrics

2. I got a gal, lives across the creek.
   Every time I look at her, my knees get weak.
   First time I tried to take her on my knee,
   She took after me with a singletree.

3. Sun's up high the Fourth of July,
   Chickens won't lay and the cow's gone dry.
   Creek's dried up, I can't go fishin'.
   Should be workin' 'stead of sittin' here wishin'.

5. Sun's comin' up, the rooster's crowin',
   Fiddler's gone, I got to be goin'
   Back to the house across the creek,
   But we'll be back at the end of the week.

BLUE BONNET LANE

Words and Music by Cindy Walker

ARKANSAS TRAVELER

Arranged and Adapted by Slim Martin

Medium Tempo

Oh, once up-on a time in Ar-kan-sas, An old man sat in his lit-tle cab-in door, And he

fid-dled at a tune that he liked to hear, A jol-ly old ___ tune that he played by ear. It was

raining hard but the fiddler didn't care, He sawed a-way at the pop-u-lar air, Though his

roof-tree leaked like a wa-ter-fall, That didn't seem to both-er the man at all.

A traveller was riding by that day,
And stopped to hear him a-fiddling away;
The cabin was afloat and his feet were wet,
But still the old man didn't seem to fret.
    So the stranger said, "Now the way it seems to me,
    You'd better mend your roof," said he.
    But the old man said as he played away:
    "I couldn't mend it now, it's a rainy day."

The traveller replied, "That's all quite true,
But this, I think is the thing for you to do;
Get busy on a day that is fair and bright,
Then patch the old roof till it's good and tight."
    But the old man kept on a-playing at his reel,
    And tapped the ground with his leathery heel.
    "Get along," said he, "for you give me a pain—
    My cabin never leaks when it doesn't rain!"

BEAUMONT RAG

Arranged and Adapted by Leonard Moss

A BIG BALL IN COWTOWN

Words and Music by Hoyle Nix

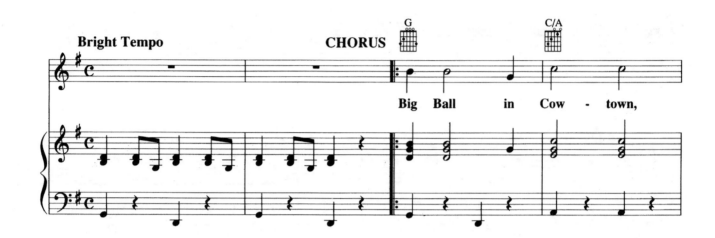

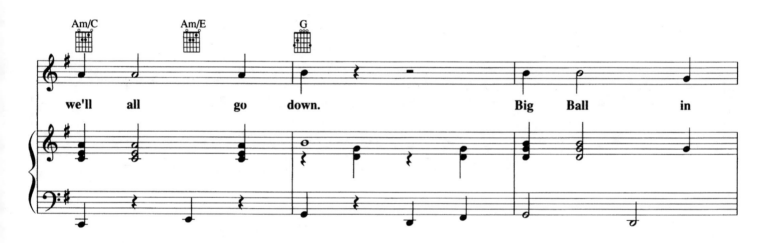

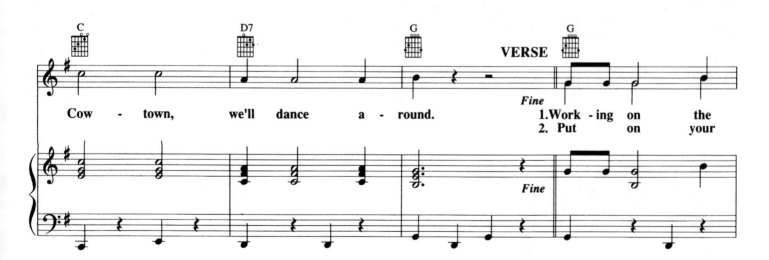

rail - road,   sleep - ing   on   the   ground.   Eat - ing
new   shoes,   put   on   your   gown.   Kick

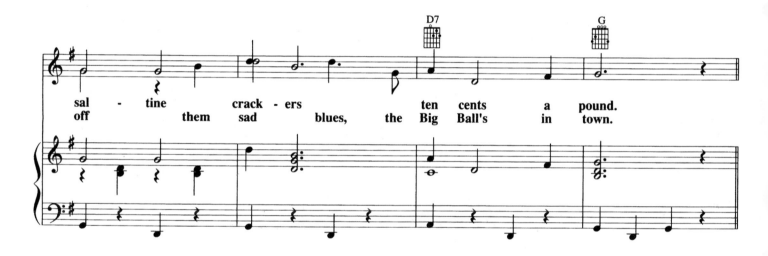

sal - tine   them   crack - ers   the   ten   cents   a   pound.
off   them   sad   blues,   the   Big   Ball's   in   town.

3. I'll stay in cow-town, I'll stick a-round
Board up your win-dows, the Big Ball's in town.
(To Chorus)

DUSTY SKIES

Words and Music by Cindy Walker

CORRINA, CORRINA

Words and Music by Sam Hopkins

EIGHT'R FROM DECATUR

By Bob Wills, Ted Powell and Dave Woody

HEART TO HEART TALK

Words and Music by Lee Ross

40

Verse 2
You smile I'll smile with you.
You cry, I'll cry for you
'cause you're the only love I've ever known.
Don't go and break my heart,
Don't say that we must part.
This world is lonely when you leave me alone.

I CAN'T GIVE YOU ANYTHING BUT LOVE

Words by Dorothy Fields
Music by Jimmy McHugh

HONEYSUCKLE ROSE

Words by Andy Razaf
Music by Thomas "Fats" Waller

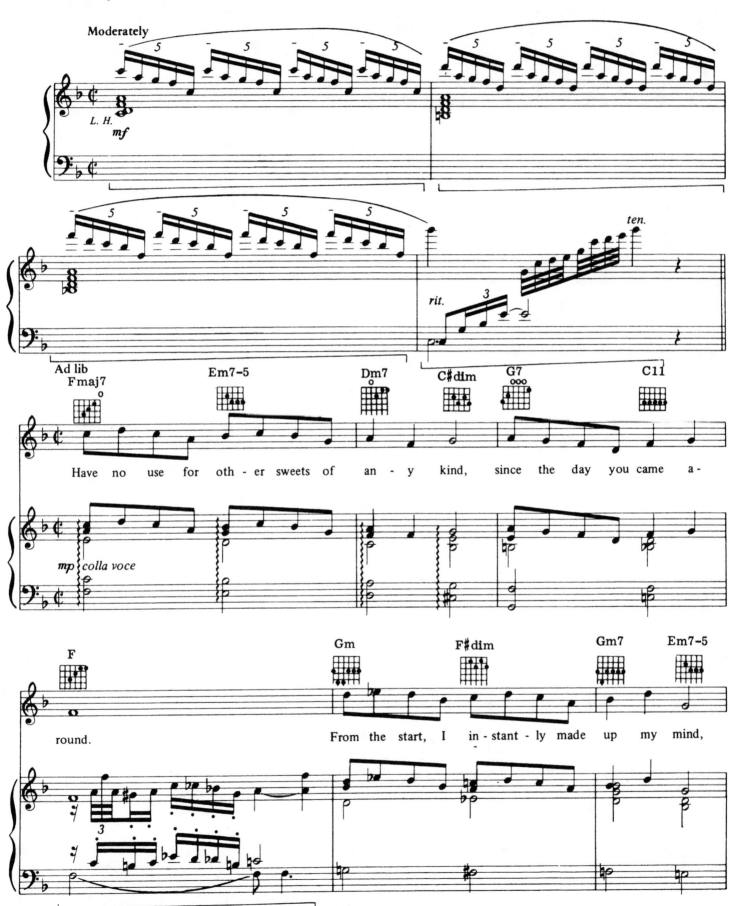

I AIN'T GOT NOBODY (And Nobody Cares For Me)

Words by Roger Graham
Music by Spencer Williams and Dave Peyton

50

I DON'T KNOW WHY

Words by Roy Turk
Music by Fred E. Ahlert

Slowly, with feeling

I NEEDED YOU

Words and Music by Bob Wills and Johnny Gimble

I KNEW THE MOMENT I LOST YOU

Words by Tommy Duncan
Music by Bob Wills

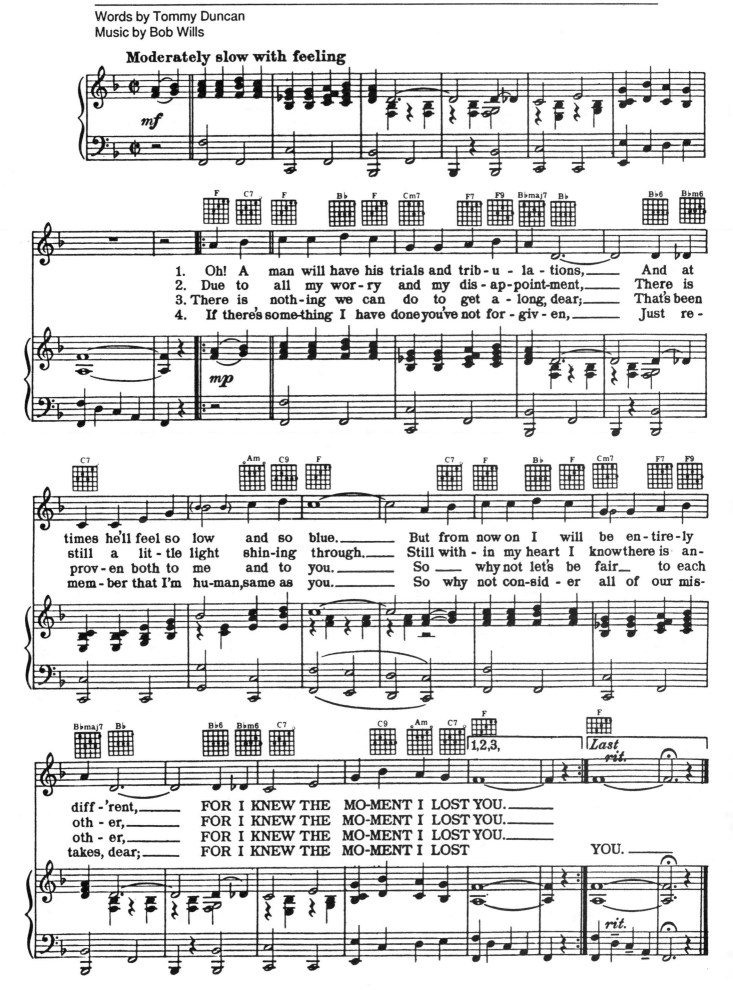

I'D LIKE TO BE IN TEXAS

Words and Music by Johnny Dollar

In a corner in an old arm chair sat a man whose hair was gray,
He had listened to them longingly, to what they had to say.
They asked him where he'd like to be and his clear old voice did ring:
"I'd like to be in Texas for the round-up in the spring.

They all sat still and listened to each word he had to say;
They knew the old man sitting there had once been young and gay.
They asked him for a story of his life out on the plains,
He slowly then removed his hat and quietly began:

"Oh, I've seen them stampede o'er the hills, when you'd think they'd never stop,
I've seen them run for miles and miles until their leader dropped,
I was foreman on a cowranch - that's the calling of a king;
I'd like to be in Texas for the round-up in the spring."

IDA RED

Arranged and Adapted by Leonard Moss

VERSE

Light the pi - lot, fire in the grate Clock on the man - tle
Lamp on the ta - ble, pic - ture on the wall There's a pret - ty soul and

says it's get - tin' late. Cur - tains on the win - dow, snow - y white
that's not all. If I'm not mis - tak - en and I'm sure I'm right, there's

Verse 3
Chicken in a bread bin pickin'out dough
Granny whatta ya know about Ohio?
Hurry up boys and don't fool around
Grab your partner and truck on down
(repeat chorus)

Verse 4
My old Missus swore to me
when she died she'd set me free
she lived so long, her head got bald
She took a notion not to die at all
(repeat chorus)

Verse 5
Repeat of verse #2
repeat chorus

LA GOLONDRINA

Words and Music by N. Sarradell

MARGIE

Words by Benny Davis
Music by Con Conrad and J.R. Robinson

MISS MOLLY

Words and Music by Cindy Walker

have you seen Miss Mol - ly? Her cheeks are ros - y red. Her
When Miss Mol - ly's smi - lin' the sun is dim a spell and
Trade my horse and sad - dle cow dri - vin' I'll re - sign if

Verse 4.
**Now listen dear Miss Molly
I've told you this before
an'even though I told you so
I'll tell you just once more**

MY WINDOW FACES THE SOUTH

Words and Music by Abner Silver, Mitchell Parish and Jerry Livingston

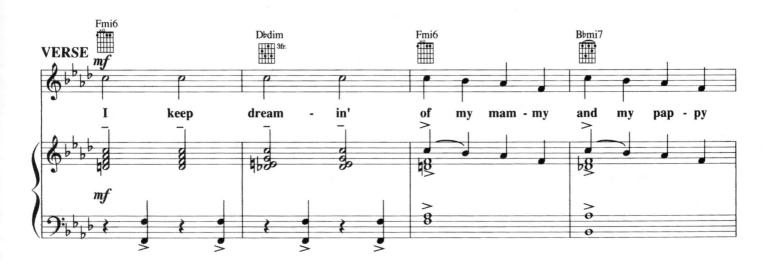

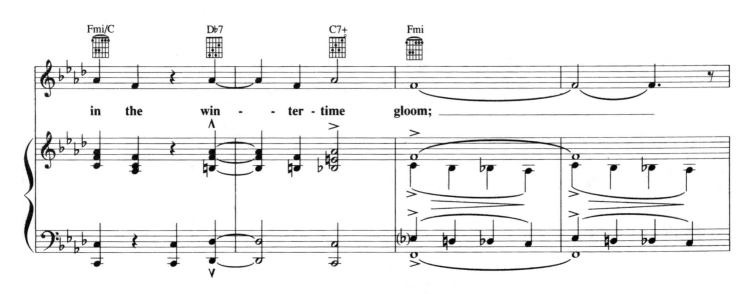

L'IL LIZA JANE

Adapted by Jimmy Murray

NIGHT LIFE

Words and Music by Willie Nelson, P. Buskirk and W. Breeland

OKLAHOMA HILLS

Words and Music by Woody Guthrie and Jack Guthrie

RED WING

Words by Thurland Chattaway
Music by Kerry Mills

1. There once lived an In-dian maid, A shy lit-tle prai-rie maid, Who
2. She watched for him day and night, She kept all the camp-fires bright, And

sang a __ lay, a love song __ gay, As on the plain she'd while a-way the day. She
un-der the sky, each night she would lie, And dream a-bout his com-ing by and by; But

loved a __ war-rior bold, this shy lit-tle maid of old, But
when all the braves re-turned, the heart of __ Red Wing yearned, For

ROLL IN MY SWEET BABY'S ARMS

Adapted by Slim Martin

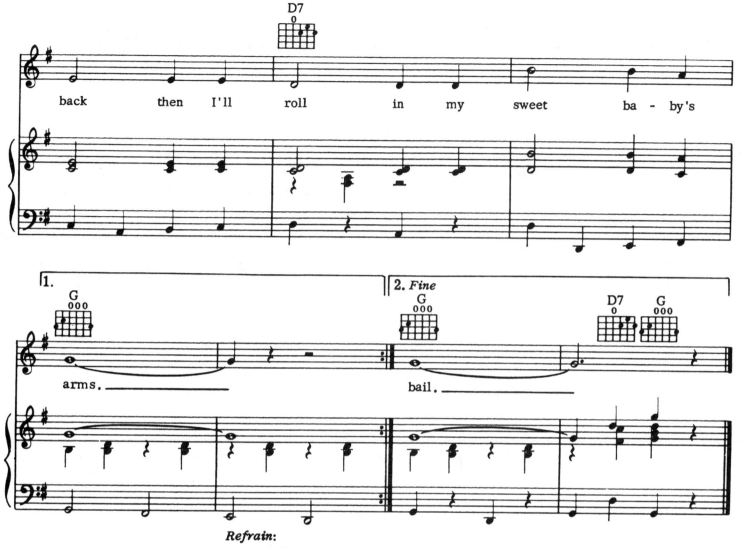

back then I'll roll in my sweet ba - by's

1.

arms.

2. *Fine*

bail.

Refrain:

Roll in my sweet baby's arms,
Roll in my sweet baby's arms,
Lay 'round the shack 'til the mail train comes back,
Then I'll roll in my sweet baby's arms.

Can't see what's the matter with my own true love,
She done quit writing to me,
She must think I don't love her like I used to,
Ain't that a foolish idea.

Sometimes there's a change in the ocean,
Sometimes there's a change in the sea,
Sometimes there's a change in my own true love,
But there's never no change in me.

Mama's a ginger-cake baker,
Sister can weave and can spin,
Dad's got an interest in that old cotton mill,
Just watch that old money roll in.

They tell me that your parents do not like me,
They have drove me away from your door,
If I had all my time to do over,
I would never go there any more.

Now where was you last Friday night,
While I was locked up in jail,
Walking the streets with another man,
Wouldn't even go my bail.

SILVER BELLS (That Ring In The Night)

By Bob Wills and Mel Stark

SINCERELY

Words and Music by Harvey Fauqua and Alan Freed

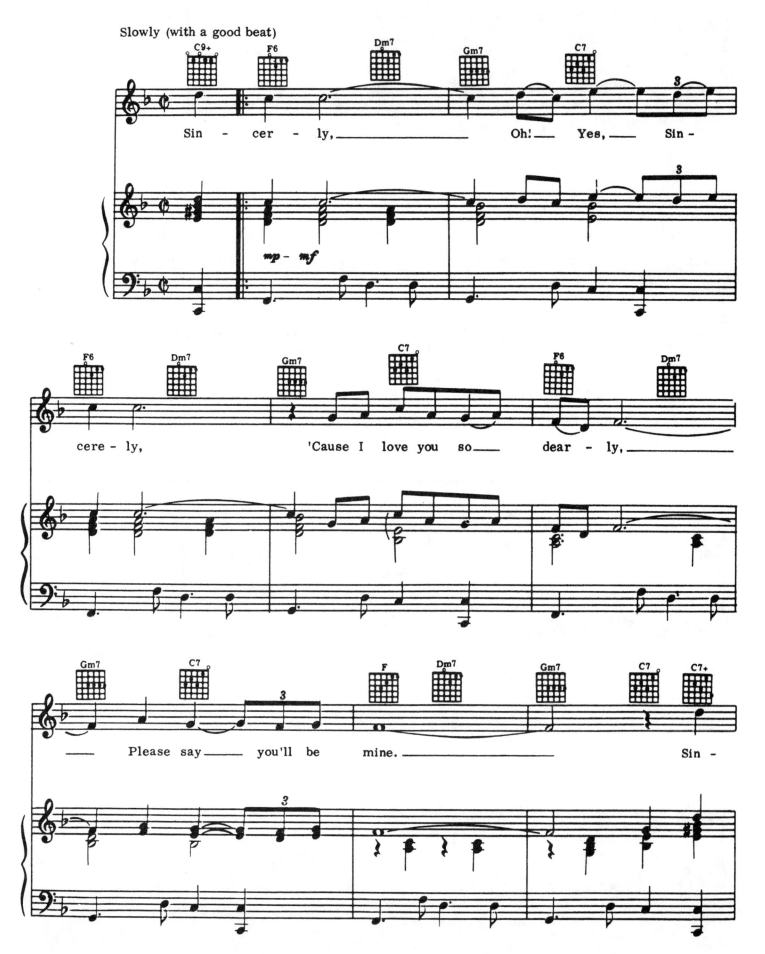

SALTY DOG

Adapted by Jesse Williams

SOMEWHERE SOUTH OF SAN ANTONE

Words and Music by Bob Wills and Johnny Gimble

SOONER OR LATER (You'll Fall)

Words and Music by Bob Wills and Artie Glenn

SOON - ER ___ OR LA - TER ___ you will fall for

some - one just the way I fell for you. ___

ST. LOUIS BLUES

Words and Music by W.C. Handy
New Arrangement by Leonard Moss

old Ken -tuck - y Col' -nel loves his rocks loves his rocks and rye, And I

love my ba - by till the day I die. ___ Got the

Saint Lou -is Blues ___ Saint Lou -is Blues ___

(in the morn -ing) *(in the eve -ning)*

ADDITIONAL CHORUS LYRICS

A black headed woman makes a freight train jump the track,
Said a black headed woman makes a freight train jump the track.
But a long tall gal makes a preacher Ball·the Jack.

Lord, a blonde headed woman makes a good man leave town,
Said a blonde headed woman makes a good man leave town.
But a red head woman makes a boy slap his papa down.

Oh, ashes to ashes and dust to dust,
I said ashes to ashes and dust to dust.
If my blues don't get you, my jazzing must.

SUNBONNET SUE

Words by Will Cobb
Music by Gus Edwards

TURKEY IN THE STRAW

Adapted by Jesse Williams

107

tur-key in the hay

roll 'em up and twist 'em up a high tuck-a-haw, and__ hit 'em up a tune__ called__

1.
"Tur-key in the Straw!" Oh I
(etc.)

2. Fine
"Tur-key in the Straw!"

Came to the river and I couldn't get across
Paid five dollars for an old blind hoss
Wouldn't go ahead, nor he wouldn't stand still
So he went up and down like an old saw mill.

As I came down the new cut road
Met Mr. Bullfrog, met Miss Toad
And every time Miss Toad would sing
Ole Bullfrog cut a pigeon wing.

Oh, I jumped in the seat, and I gave a little yell,
The horses run away, broke the wagon all to hell;
Sugar in the gourd and honey in the horn,
I never was so happy since the hour I was born.

UNDER THE DOUBLE EAGLE

By Josef Wagner

WILL THE CIRCLE BE UNBROKEN?

Words and Music by Sarah Mills

TIME CHANGES EVERYTHING

Words and Music by Tommy Duncan

Moderately

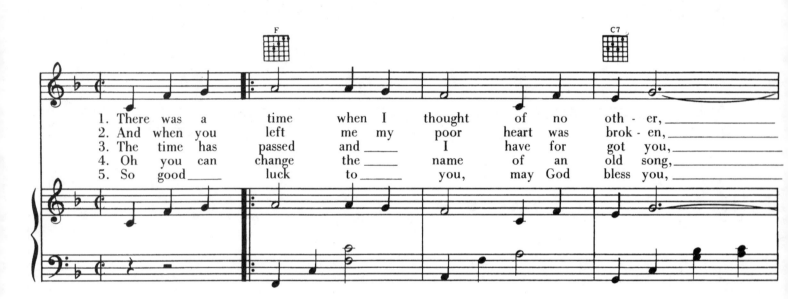

1. There was a time when I thought of no oth-er,
2. And when you left me my poor heart was brok-en,
3. The time has passed and I have for got you,
4. Oh you can change the name of an old song,
5. So good luck to you, may God bless you,

And we sang our own love's re-frain,
Our ro-mance seemed all in vain,
Moth-er Na-ture does won-der-ful things,
Re-ar-range it and make it swing,
I can't say we won't love a-gain,

THE YELLOW ROSE OF TEXAS

Adapted by Woody Hayes

WHO'S SORRY NOW?

Words by Bert Kalmar and Harry Ruby
Music by Ted Snyder

WHERE DO I GO FROM HERE?

Words and Music by Bob Wills and Edgar Rauch

Slow Waltz

Man - y years a - go   I fell for you   with heart and   soul,   I ded - i -
I have pon - dered this   af - ter ev' - ry good - night kiss   and the

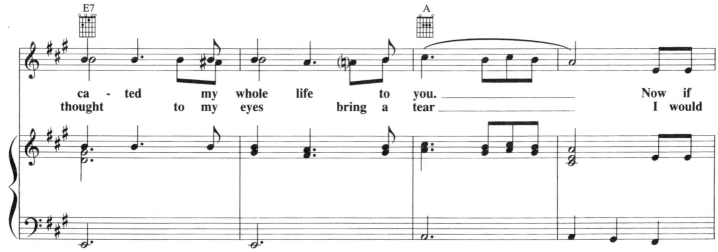

ca - ted   my whole life   to you. _____   Now if
thought   to my eyes   bring a tear _____   I would

BACK HOME AGAIN IN INDIANA

Words by Ballard MacDonald
Music by James F. Hanley

COTTON-EYED JOE (Two-step)

Traditional

Mod-Fast
Square Dance Tempo

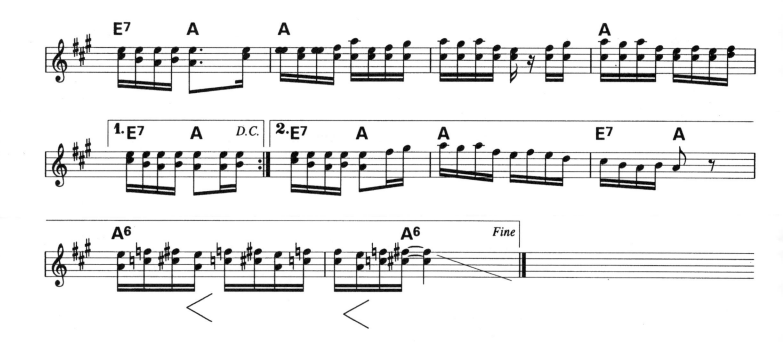

Hey my grand mammy did you know?
The chicken in the bread pan's Cotton-Eyed Joe.

cho: Where'd you come from, where did you go?
Where'd you come from, Cotton-Eyed Joe?
Where'd you come from, where did you go?
Where'd you come from, Cotton-Eyed Joe?

I'd been married fourty years ago,
If it hadn't been for Cotton-Eyed Joe.

Chorus

Get down the fiddle and rosin up the bow,
Play a little tune called Cotton-Eyed Joe.

Chorus

This version of Cotton-Eyed Joe is played mainly in Texas and out west. However, it is gaining popularity nationwide, being played to the two step. Note the different variations in letter B to letter C, along with the E note drone. Also note the different variations in measures 5, 6 and 7 of letters C and D, using the C# drone. In Texas, this is the version where everyone hollers and stomps their boots while they dance the "Texas 2 Step".

THE GIRL I LEFT BEHIND ME

Traditional

LOVESICK BLUES

Words and Music by Cliff Friend and Irving Mills

128

STAY A LITTLE LONGER

Words and Music by Tommy Duncan

With Vigor

1. You ought to see my blue - eyed Sal - ly, She lives a - way down on
2. You cain't get home if you're go - in' by the mill, 'Cause the bridge washed out at the
3. — Set - tin' in the win - dow, Sing - in' to my love, __ A trash buck - et fell from the
4. — Grab your gal and pat her on the head, __ If she don't like bis - cuits

Shin - bone al - ley; The num-ber on the gate, the num-ber on the door And the
bot - tom of the hill; The big creek's up and the big creek's lev - el,
win - dow up a - bove; — Mule and a grass - hop - per eat - in' ice - cream, And the
feed her corn bread, The girls on big creek a - bout half grown, jump

TAKE ME BACK TO TULSA

Words and Music by Bob Wills and Tommy Duncan

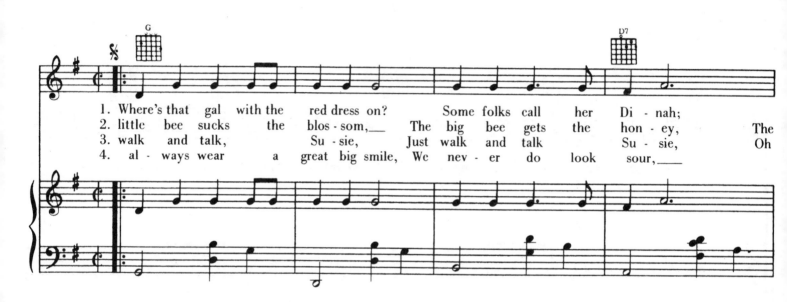

1. Where's that gal with the red dress on? Some folks call her Di - nah;
2. little bee sucks the blos - som,___ The big bee gets the hon - ey, The
3. walk and talk, Su - sie, Just walk and talk Su - sie, Oh
4. al - ways wear a great big smile, We nev - er do look sour,___

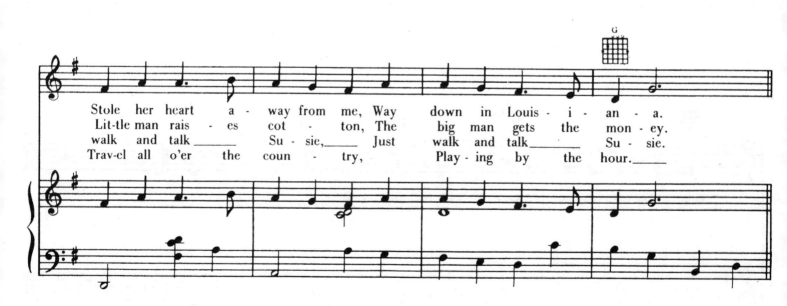

Stole her heart a - way from me, Way down in Louis - i - an - a.
Lit - tle man rais - es cot - ton, The big man gets the mon - ey.
walk and talk____ Su - sie,____ Just walk and talk____ Su - sie.
Trav-el all o'er the coun - try, Play - ing by the hour.____